HBJ Reading Program

Margaret Early

Bernice E. Cullinan
Roger C. Farr
W. Dorsey Hammond
Nancy Santeusanio
Dorothy S. Strickland

LEVEL 5

Smiles

HBJ **HARCOURT BRACE JOVANOVICH, PUBLISHERS**
Orlando   San Diego   Chicago   Dallas

Acknowledgments

For permission to reprint copyrighted material, grateful acknowledgment is made to the following sources:

Coward, McCann & Geoghegan: Adapted from *The Helping Day* by Ann Bixby Herold. Text copyright © 1980 by Ann Bixby Herold.

E. P. Dutton, a division of New American Library: "The Little Elf" from *St. Nicholas Book of Verse* by John Kendrick Bangs. Copyright 1923, 1951 by John Kendrick Bangs. A Hawthorn book.

Four Winds Press, an imprint of Macmillan Publishing Company: Adapted from "A New Friend" in *Margie and Me* by Beverly Wirth. Text copyright © 1983 by Beverly Wirth.

Greenwillow Books, a division of William Morrow & Company, Inc.: Play adaptation of *The Strongest One of All* by Mirra Ginsburg. Copyright © 1977 by Mirra Ginsburg.

Harper & Row, Publishers, Inc.: Complete text, abridged and adapted, from *Ottie and the Star* and illustrations by Laura Jean Allen. Copyright © 1979 by Laura Jean Allen. Complete text, abridged and adapted, and illustrations from "Little Bear and Emily" in *Little Bear's Friend,* written by Else Holmelund Minarik, illustrated by Maurice Sendak. Text copyright © 1960 by Else Holmelund Minarik; pictures copyright © 1960 by Maurice Sendak. Abridged from pp. 1–2 in *Listen, Rabbit* by Aileen Fisher. Copyright © 1964 by Aileen Fisher. Published by Thomas Y. Crowell. Text and illustrations from "The Kite" in *Days With Frog and Toad* by Arnold Lobel. Copyright © 1979 by Arnold Lobel. Complete text, abridged and adapted, and specified illustrations from *Owly,* written by Mike Thaler and illustrated by David Wiesner. Text copyright © 1982 by Michael C. Thaler; illustrations copyright © 1982 by David Wiesner. "Hippo Paints a Picture," abridged and adapted, from *It's Me Hippo* by Mike Thaler. Copyright © 1983 by Michael C. Thaler. Complete text, abridged and adapted, and illustrations from "A Fish Story" (Retitled: "Pelly and Peak") in *Pelly and Peak,* written and illustrated by Sally Wittman. Copyright © 1978 by Sally Christensen Wittman.

Florence M. Harrison, as Conservator to Edward W. Field: From *I Wonder . . . About the Sky* (Titled: "I Wonder") by Enid Field. Copyright © 1973 by Regensteiner Publishing Enterprises, Inc.

Random House, Inc.: "Stars" from *The Joan Walsh Anglund Story Book* by Joan Walsh Anglund. Copyright © 1978 by Joan Walsh Anglund. Adapted from *A Little at a Time* by David Adler, illustrated by N. M. Bodecker. Text copyright © 1976 by David Adler; illustrations copyright © 1976 by N. M. Bodecker.

USDA Forest Service, P. O. Box 2417, Room 1001 RP-E, Washington, DC 20013: Adapted from the *Smokey Bear Program* (Titled: "Smokey the Bear" by Jane B. Wetham).

Key: (l) – Left; (r) – Right; (c) – Center; (t) – Top; (b) – Bottom

Photographs

Cover: John Putnam/DPI

Page 2, HBJ Photo/P.C. and Connie Peri; 3 (l), Walsh Bellville/Frozen Images; 3 (r), D. Cody/FPG; 17, Photri, Inc.; 49, D. Cody/FPG; 52, Ed Cooper; 53, A. & L. Hoglund/H. Armstrong Roberts; 68, NASA; 69, Alan Carey/The Image Works; 70, Dan McCoy/Rainbow; 71 (tl), Breck P. Kent/Imagery; 71 (tr), Breck P. Kent/Imagery; 71(bc), NASA from Photri, Inc.; 72, HBJ Photo/Beverly Brosius; 82, HBJ Photo; 83 (t), HBJ Photo; 83 (b), Doug Wechsler; 84, HBJ Photo; 85, HBJ Photo/Rodney Jones; 86, HBJ Photo/Rodney Jones; 97, A. & L. Hoglund/H. Armstrong Roberts; 100, H. Armstrong Roberts; 101 (l), H. Armstrong Roberts; 101 (r), Mickey Pfleger; 141, Alexander Calder. *The Circus.* (1926 - 31). Mixed media, includes; wire, wood, metal, cloth, paper, leather, string, rubber tubing, corks, buttons, sequins, nuts and bolts and bottle caps. 54 × 94 ¼ × 94 ¼ inches. Collection of Whitney Museum of American Art. Purchase, with funds from a public fundraising campaign in May 1982. One half the funds were contributed by the Robert Wood Johnson Jr. Charitable Trust. Additional major donations were given by The Lauder Foundation; the Robert Lehman Foundation, Inc.; the Howard and Jean Lipman Foundation, Inc.; an anonymous donor; The T.M. Evans Foundation, Inc.; MacAndrews & Forbes Group, Incorporated; the De Witt Wallace Fund; Martin and Agneta Gruss; Anne Phillips; Mr. and Mrs. Laurence S. Rockefeller; the Simon Foundation, Inc.; Marylou Whitney; Bankers Trust Company; Mr. and Mrs. Kenneth N. Dayton; Joel and Anne Ehrenkranz; Irvin and Kenneth Feld; Flora Whitney Miller. More than 500 individuals from 26 states and abroad also contributed to the campaign. 83.36; 142 (l), Pedro E. Guerrero; 142 (r), Mario Paluan/Art Resource; 143 (t), Pedro E. Guerrero; 143 (b), Contour Plowing, 1974, Gouache. 29 ¼ × 43 ⅛ inches, Collection of Whitney Museum of American Art, Gift of the Artist; 144 (l), Robert H. Glaze,/Artstreet; 144 (r), Inge Morath/Magnum Photos; 147, H. Armstrong Roberts; 150-151, HBJ Photo/Paul Gerding; 168, Breck P. Kent/Imagery; 207, HBJ Photo/Paul Gerding

Contents: Unit 1, 2–3, Walsh Belville/Frozen Images; Unit 2, 53, A. & L. Hoglund/H. Armstrong Roberts; Unit 3, 101, Mickey Pfleger; Unit 4, 150–151, HBJ Photo/Paul Gerding.

Illustrators

Lynn Uhde Adams: 158-159; Laura Jean Allen: 74-78; Cheryl Arnemann: 174-182; Dave Blanchette: 122-126; N.M. Bodecker: 160-166; Jesse Clay: 38-39, 128-129, 152-156; Tom Dunnington: 12-16, 18; Len Ebert: 184-188; Ethel Gold: 41-46, 102-108, 169-172, 190-193; Meryl Henderson: 4-10; Arnold Lobel: 194-204; Mary McLaren: 210-224; Jan Palmer: 66-67; Jan Pyke: 130-138; Monica Santa: 80-81; Maurice Sendek: 20-26; John Slobodnik: 64-65, 140; Jerry Smath: 110-118, 120-121; David Wiesner: 54-62; Bernard Wiseman: 28-36; Sally Wittman: 88-94.

Printed in the United States of America

ISBN 0-15-330505-3

Contents

Unit 2 Land and Sea 52

He saw the green hills.
He saw the river.
Far, far away he saw the blue sea.
He saw the tops of trees.
He saw his house.
He saw Mother Bear.

He began to climb down the tree.

On the way down he saw a little green worm.

"Hello," said the little green worm. "Talk to me."

"I will talk some other time," said Little Bear.

"Now I must go home for lunch."

Little Bear climbed all the way down the tree.

There he saw a little girl.

"I think I am lost," said the
little girl.

"Could you see the river from
the treetop?"

"Oh, yes," said Little Bear.
"I could see the river.
Do you live there?"

"Yes," said the little girl.
"My name is Emily."

"I am Little Bear.
I can take you to the river."

So, Little Bear and Emily walked
and talked together.
Soon they came to the river.

"I see my mother and father,"
said Emily.

"My mother is calling," said
Little Bear.
"I must go home for lunch.
Good-bye, Emily."

"Good-bye, Little Bear.
Come and play with me again."

"I will," said Little Bear.

Little Bear went home.

He hugged Mother Bear and asked,
"Do you know what I just did?"

"What did you just do, Little Bear?"
asked Mother Bear.

"I climbed to the top of a tree,
and I saw the wide world.

I saw the blue sea," said Little Bear.
"And on the way down, I saw a
little green worm.

I climbed all the way down," he said.
"Then what do you think I saw?"

"What did you see?" asked
Mother Bear.

"I saw a little girl named Emily,"
said Little Bear.
"She was lost, so I helped her
to get home.
Now I have a new friend.
Who do you think it is?"

"The little green worm," laughed
Mother Bear.

Little Bear laughed too.
"No," he said, "it is Emily.
Emily and I are friends."

1. What did Little Bear find in the story?

2. Why did Emily need help?

3. How did Little Bear help Emily?

4. How do you know that Emily wants to see Little Bear again?

5. What makes you think Little Bear and his mother have fun together?

Someone has sent letters but didn't sign them.
Read to find out who sent the letters.

The Surprise Letters

story and pictures by Bernard Wiseman

"Eddie, here is a letter for you,"
his mother said.

"Who is it from?" asked Eddie.

"Open it and see," she said.

"It must be from one of my best
friends," said Eddie, as he opened
his letter.

"This is funny!" Eddie laughed.

"I have read this letter, but I still don't know who sent it!"

"Isn't there a name on it?" his mother asked.

"The letter isn't signed, but someone drew a funny face on it!" said Eddie.

"I'll read the letter to you."

Dear Eddie,
Find out
who I am!
My name
has an i
in it. ☺

"Nina has an *i* in her name," said Eddie's mother.

"Linda and Tim have an *i* in their names, too," said Eddie.

"So do Rick and Kim!" his mother said.

"All my best friends have an *i* in their names," said Eddie.
"I'll find out who sent this letter!
I'm going to see my friends now."

Eddie rode his bike to Nina's
house.

His friends were there, playing.

"Who sent me a letter and didn't
sign it?" asked Eddie.

"Oh," said Tim, "you got
one, too!

We all thought that you were
the one who sent letters to us!

We thought you were the one who
drew the funny faces on our letters."

"I rode my bike over here to find
out who sent my letter," said Linda.

"I thought Eddie did it.

Now I still don't know who
sent it."

"I'll find out who did it,"
thought Eddie.

Eddie said, "Tim, show us
your letter."
Tim showed his letter.

"Linda, show us your letter,"
said Eddie.
Linda showed her letter.

"Kim, show us your letter,"
said Eddie.

Kim didn't have a letter to show.
She just looked down at the grass
and smiled.

"You didn't get a letter, did you?
Are you the one who sent all the
letters?" asked Eddie.

"Yes, I'm the one," said Kim.
"I thought I would surprise you."

"You did surprise us, Kim.
Now we all know who sent the
letters," laughed Eddie.
"You are funny, Kim!"

Kim laughed.
All her friends laughed, too.

1. Who sent the letters but didn't sign them?

2. Who got the letters?

3. What clue did Eddie have in his letter?

4. On page 35, how did Eddie know that Kim wrote the letters?

5. Do you think the children liked their surprise letters? How do you know?

Ottie wanted to show the star
to her mother.

Ottie took the star up to the
top of the water.

"Look, Mother! I found a star!"
said Ottie.

"That is not a star, Ottie,"
said her mother.
"It's a starfish."

"It looks like a star," said Ottie.

"I know," said her mother,
"but stars are up in the sky.
Starfish live down under the water."

"I want to go home!"
said the starfish.

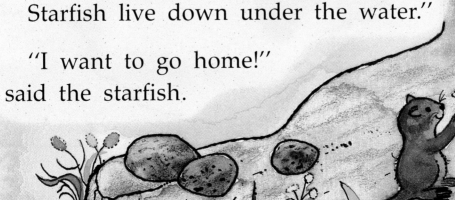

"I'll take you home," said Ottie.

"I know my way home," said
the starfish.

Ottie put the starfish back into
the water.

"Good-bye, Starfish," said Ottie.

"Good-bye, Ottie," called
the starfish.

Ottie and her mother waved
as the starfish swam
down under the water.

1. What did Ottie learn about the stars?

2. Why did Ottie jump into the water?

3. What kind of star did she find in the water?

4. What did Ottie's mother teach Ottie?

5. How did you know the starfish was sad?

Stars

by Joan Walsh Anglund

The star looked down
  at the deep, dark sea
And he thought to himself,
  "Is that a twin to me,
Shining so brightly, there below?"

And he pondered,
  and then he decided, "No,
That couldn't be true,
  for I'm so high.
. . . And, besides, all *stars*
  live up in the sky!"

And the starfish, below,
   looked up to the sky.
"Why, that's a brother of mine,
   pinned up so high!"
But then he thought,
   "How could that be,

For everyone knows
   stars live in the sea!"
So both stars fell asleep,
   each in his blue,
And neither one questioned
   . . . so neither one knew!

Many people work at a marine park.
Read to find out what their jobs are.

At a Marine Park

by Carl Donneley

If you went to a marine park,
you could see many sea animals.
You could see starfish, sharks,
dolphins, and otters.

Many people work at a marine park.
The animals must be fed.
Their homes must be cleaned.
Some of the marine park animals
must be trained for shows.

This is Margie.
Her job is to feed the starfish.
Margie feeds plants and little fish to the starfish.

Starfish don't eat the same way that people eat.

People put food into their mouths.

A starfish pushes its stomach outside its mouth.

It puts its stomach over its food.

Then the starfish eats the food with its stomach.

Here is Robert.

He takes care of the sharks.

One of his jobs is to clean the shark tank.

First a net is dropped into the water.

The net keeps the sharks on one side of the tank.

Then Robert jumps into the water on the other side.

Next he cleans that side of the tank.

Here are Tim and Rita.

Tim and Rita train the dolphins.

They teach the dolphins to do many things.

The dolphins learn to jump out of the water.

The dolphins learn to come when they are called.

They learn to play ball.

Tim and Rita learn how to ride on the backs of the dolphins.

This is Nina.

She trains the otters.

It takes a long time to train
the otters.

The otters learn to play ball.

They learn to clap.

Nina, Tim, and Rita like training
sea animals.

Margie and Robert like their jobs,
too.

Someday, you may want to work
at a marine park, too.

1. What are some of the jobs people do in a marine park?

2. What can dolphins and otters be trained to do?

3. What makes you think that people and animals learn at a marine park?

4. Why are the people who work at the marine park so happy?

5. What job would you like to do in a marine park?

Peak the peacock can do something very well on land. Pelly the pelican can do something very well in the sea. What can these two birds do?

Pelly and Peak

story and pictures by Sally Wittman

Pelly and Peak were by the sea.
"What a fine day it is!" said Peak.
"I feel like opening my fan!
Close your eyes, Pelly."

Pelly closed his eyes.
"Now open your eyes," said Peak.

"You look like a rainbow!"
said Pelly.

"It was nothing," said Peak.
"All peacocks look like this."

"I wish that I looked like a
peacock," said Pelly, "but pelicans
are not so fancy."

"Don't be sad," said Peak.
"I'll find a way to cheer
you up."

Peak sat on a log to think.
"I know," said Peak.
"We can go fishing!"

"Good!" said Pelly.
Pelly went into the water.
He began to swim.

"You forgot your fishing pole,"
called Peak.

"I never use one," said Pelly.

"Be careful," called Peak.
"The water is deep."

"Yes, the water is deep,
but I can swim very well.
　Are you coming in?" called Pelly.

　"No, thank you," said Peak.
"I never swim.
I will fish from the land."

Peak put a worm on his hook.
Then he dropped the hook into
the water.
　He waited for a fish to bite.

The sun was so hot that Peak
went to sleep.

A fish began to eat Peak's worm.

The fish pulled on the pole.

Then the fish swam away
with the worm and the hook
and the pole.

This woke Peak up.

"Come back with my pole,"
Peak shouted to the fish.

Then Peak saw Pelly coming
out of the water.

"A fish took my pole!" Peak
cried.

"Did you get a fish?"

Pelly opened his bill.
He dropped some fish on the
sand.

"Good work!" said Peak.

"It was nothing," said Pelly.
"Fishing is easy for a pelican."

"You see," said Peak, "we are
both good at some things."

"Yes, and we are not so good
at others," laughed Pelly.

Pelly and Peak went home.
They both felt good inside.

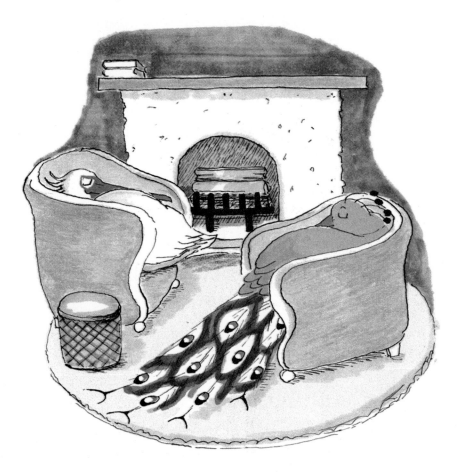

1. What could Pelly and Peak do?

2. What did Pelly and Peak learn?

3. When in the story did you know that Peak wanted Pelly to be happy?

4. How can you tell that Pelly and Peak were good friends?

5. What did you like about this story?

Thinking About "Land and Sea"

In "Land and Sea," you met people and animals who asked questions about the world.

Owly asked questions about the stars, the sky, and the sea.

Ottie learned about stars and starfish.

What things did the people and animals learn at a marine park?

Pelly and Peak learned something very special.

What did Pelly and Peak learn?

What did you learn about the world from reading "Land and Sea"?

What questions do you still have?

Where do you think you can find the answers?

1. Name some things that you read about that happened on the land. Name some things that happened in the sea.

2. What job from the stories "People Who Ask Questions" and "At a Marine Park" would you like to have?

3. How did Pelly, Peak, and Owly find out that they were special?

4. What were some of the same questions asked by Owly, Ottie, and people who ask questions?

Read on Your Own

Peterkin Meets a Star by Emilie Boon. Random House. What happens when a boy pulls a star out of the sky and takes it home?

The Sky Is Full of Stars by Franklyn M. Branley. Harper. This book tells how to find special stars and star pictures in the sky.

The Chick and the Duckling by Mirra Ginsburg. Macmillan. Find out what happens when a chick wants to do everything a duckling does.

Little Owl, Keeper of the Trees by Ronald and Ann Himler. Harper. This book has three stories about the adventures of a young owl.

Owliver by Robert Kraus. Dutton. Owliver doesn't know what he should be when he grows up.

Swimmy by Leo Lionni. Pantheon. One smart little fish shows some other little fish a good trick.

The Moon and the Balloon by Mike Thaler. Hastings. Read about a balloon who wants to be like the moon.

More Tales of Oliver Pig by Jean Van Leeuwen. Dial. The story "Questions" is one of the four stories about Oliver Pig in this book.

Unit 3
Smiles

It feels good to smile.

It feels good to make others smile.

In "Smiles," you will see how a little boy helps some animals.

You will see how some friends help each other.

As you read, look for people and animals who help others.

Read to find out what makes some people and animals smile.

*What kind of day does
David have?
What does he do that makes
his father smile?*

The Helping Day

by Ann Bixby Herold

It was a nice day.
David felt good all over.
He felt like helping others.
His father was painting the house.
"I'll help you, Dad," said David.

"Not now, David," said his father.
"This is hard work."

David's brother was making
an airplane.
"I'll help you, Mike," said David.

"No thanks," said Mike.

David went over to his mother.
She was cutting the grass.
"Mother, please let me help you
cut the grass," said David.

"There's nothing more to do,"
said his mother.

David felt sad.
"Why can't I help?" he thought.

David sat on the back steps
and ate a cracker.

Cracker crumbs dropped down
as he ate.

Some ants came and started taking
the crumbs to an anthill.

At last there was just one large
crumb.

It was too large for the ants
to move.

"I'll help you," said David.

David pushed the large cracker
crumb to the anthill with a stick.

The ants took it down into
the anthill.

"Good-bye, ants," said David.

David got up from the back steps.
He walked down a path near
his house.
He saw a worm on the path.
"You'll be stepped on if you stay
on that path!" David said to
the worm.

David used his stick to move
the worm back into the grass.
He found more worms on the path.
He moved them all with the stick.
"Stay off the path, worms,"
David said.

David walked back to his house.

He saw something move near
a door.

He went to see what it was.

He saw a butterfly in an old web.

David broke the old web with his
stick.

He took the butterfly out of the
web and let it go.

"Good-bye, butterfly," called David.

"David? David?" called his father.
"I thought you wanted to help."

"Make him help with the work,"
said David's brother.
"He hasn't helped all day."

"Yes I have," said David.
"Come and see, Dad."

David showed his father the anthill, the worms, and the web.

"I gave some cracker crumbs to the ants and moved some worms. I helped a butterfly, too," said David.

David's father smiled. "That's a lot of helping," said his father. "You must want something to eat. I'll go and get some food for us."

"Will you get something for Mike and Mother, too?" asked David.

"Yes," said his father.

David smiled and said, "Good, then I'll help."

1. What kind of day did David have?

2. What did David do that made his father smile?

3. What did Father and David do together?

4. How did you feel about David's brother saying, "He hasn't helped all day"?

5. When did David stop feeling sad?

Mama Fig is not happy in her house on the hill. How do Mr. Fig and his friends make her happy?

Mama Fig's House

by Elizabeth K. Cooper

These are people who are needed for the play.

Narrator	**Mr. Fig**	**Rabbit**
Owl	**Mama Fig**	**Mouse**
Turtle	**Red Hen**	

Narrator: Mr. Fig and his friends
 are going to see Mama Fig.
 Their laughter is heard as they fly
 higher and higher in the Figmobile.

Owl: Oh, Mr. Fig, I like to ride
 in your Figmobile.
 It's so much fun!

Turtle: Look! It's starting to rain.
 When will we get to
 Mama Fig's house?

Mr. Fig: There it is now.
 Keep your magic hats
 on, everyone.
 The magic hats will help us land
 the Figmobile.

Narrator: The Figmobile lands
at the top of a hill.

Mama Fig: Hello, Son!
I heard laughter.
So I came out to see
who was laughing.
I'm so glad to see you.
How is everyone?
Come in before you all get wet.

Narrator: Mr. Fig and the animals
go into Mama Fig's house.
All but Rabbit take their hats
into the house.

Red Hen: I'm glad we're inside your
house, Mama Fig.
It's raining so hard!

Rabbit: Do you like living
on top of this hill, Mama Fig?

Mama Fig: I *should* like it here,
but I don't.
All my friends live at the bottom
of the hill.

Red Hen: Perhaps we can help you
find a new house.

Mama Fig: Oh no, Red Hen!
I don't want a new house.
I'd just like to move this house
to the bottom of the hill.

Mr. Fig: That will be hard to do.
Perhaps we could use our magic
hats, Mama.

Narrator: When the rain stopped, all the animals but Rabbit put on their magic hats.

Rabbit: I left my hat in the Figmobile.
I must get it.

Owl: Be careful, Rabbit!
It has rained hard outside.
The road should be very muddy by now.

Narrator: Rabbit is heard shouting for help.

Mouse: That's Rabbit shouting.
Look! He's sliding down the
muddy hill.
I'll get his hat from the
Figmobile.

Narrator: Mouse gets Rabbit's hat.
He helps Rabbit back to the house.
Everyone sees that Rabbit is fine.

Mr. Fig: I'm not happy that you slid
down the hill, Rabbit.
But you just gave me a good idea!
Perhaps we can slide Mama Fig's
house down the muddy hill.
Our magic hats will help us
push the house.

Mouse: All we need to do is give the house a little push. Our magic hats and the mud should do the hard work.

Narrator: So they all push the house.
The house starts to slide down the muddy hill.
At last the house stops at the bottom of the hill.

Turtle: We did it!
Rabbit gave Mr. Fig a good idea.
Our magic hats and the mud helped us!

Mama Fig: I'm so happy!
Now I can be with my friends.
Thank you, everyone!

Mr. Fig: Mama, I must get
the Figmobile now.
I have to take my friends
to their homes.

Narrator: Mr. Fig gets the
Figmobile.
He rides down to the
bottom of the hill.
His friends and Mama Fig
wait outside for him.

Mr. Fig: Good-bye, Mama.
I'm so glad we could help you.
Climb in, everyone.
We have to go now.

Animals: Good-bye, Mama Fig!

Mama Fig: Good-bye!
Thanks again for all your help.

Narrator: Mama Fig's laughter is
heard as the friends fly higher
into the sky.
Mama Fig is very happy.
The friends are happy, too!

1. How did Mr. Fig and his friends make Mama Fig happy?

2. Why didn't Mama Fig like living at the top of the hill?

3. What was Mr. Fig's good idea?

4. What gave Mr. Fig the idea?

5. Who tells the story when no one is talking?

Main Idea

Look at the picture below.
Then read what Mouse and Rabbit
are saying about the picture.
Who is telling the main idea?

Rabbit is telling the main idea
of the picture.
Mouse is only telling about
a small part of the picture.

Now look at the other two pictures.
Tell which animal is saying
the main idea in each picture.

Do you think this story about why rabbits have long ears is true? Why? Why not?

Why Rabbits Have Long Ears

retold by Valery Carrick

Long ago there was a rabbit who made friends with a sheep. The sheep and the rabbit played together.

They did everything together. The sheep and the rabbit were very good friends.

One day the sheep said,
"Let's build a house!"

"Yes!" said the rabbit.
"Let's build a house."

So they went into the forest to get some logs to build a house.
The sheep saw a tall tree.

"I can push this tree down!" said the sheep.

"You cannot!" said the rabbit.

"Oh, yes I can," said the sheep.
"I'll show you!"

The sheep took a long run.
He hit the tree with his head.
The tree crashed down!
"You did it!" said the rabbit.
"Now I know how to push
down a tree, too."

Soon they saw another tall tree.
"I bet I can make that tree
come crashing down!" said
the rabbit.

"You cannot!" said the sheep.

"Oh, yes I can," said the rabbit.
"I'll show you!"

The rabbit took a long run.

He hit the tree so hard that his head went into his shoulders.

The tree did not come crashing down.

"Rabbit! Your head went into your shoulders!" said the sheep.

"I will help you."

The sheep put the rabbit's short ears into his mouth and started to pull.

He pulled as hard as he could.

"Stop! Stop pulling my short ears!" the rabbit shouted.

But the sheep went on pulling. At last the rabbit's head came out of his shoulders.

"You just about pulled my ears out of my head!" said the rabbit.

"Look! Look what you did to my short ears.

Now they are very long."

"Yes, your ears are very long," laughed the sheep.

So now you know why rabbits have long ears!

1. Do you think this story about why rabbits have long ears is true? Why?

2. Why did the rabbit's head go down into his shoulders?

3. What made you laugh in this story?

4. When was the first time in the story that you knew that the rabbit would have long ears?

5. Which character in the story did you like best? Tell why.

Listen, Rabbit

by Aileen Fisher

I saw him first
when the sun went down
in the summer sky
at the edge of town
where grass grew green
and the path grew brown.

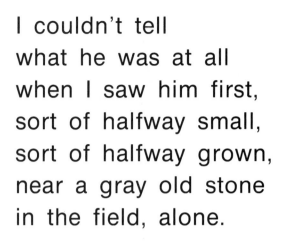

I couldn't tell
what he was at all
when I saw him first,
sort of halfway small,
sort of halfway grown,
near a gray old stone
in the field, alone.

Then I saw his ears
standing rabbit tall!

My heart went thump!
And do you know why?
'Cause I hoped that maybe
as time went by
the rabbit and I
(if he felt like *me*)
could have each other
for company.

Hippo paints a picture.
Why does he have a hard
time painting the picture?

Hippo Paints a Picture

by Mike Thaler

It was a pretty morning.
Hippo was in the river.
The sky was bright blue.
The sun was bright yellow.

"I think I will paint a
picture," he said.
He climbed out of the river
and went to town.

130

Hippo got some yellow, red, blue, and white paint.

He got a brush and a cap.

He put on his cap and walked back home.

Then he started to paint.

He painted all morning.

By lunchtime, he had painted the grass, the tree, the hill, the sky and the sun.

"After lunch I will paint the flowers.
Then my picture will be finished,"
said Hippo.

Hippo ran home to eat his lunch.
Then he ran back and painted
the flowers.

"There," he smiled.
"I am finished."

Snake came to see Hippo's picture.

"It does not look finished to me," said Snake.
"You did not put in that cloud."

"It was not there this morning," said Hippo.

"Well, it is there now," said Snake.

"All right," said Hippo.
He put some white paint on his brush and painted the cloud.

"Now it is finished," said Hippo.

"Not quite," said Snake.
"A robin just landed on that tree."

"All right, all right," said Hippo.
"I will put him in."

Hippo painted the robin.
"Now my painting is perfect,"
he said.

"Not quite," said Snake, moving next
to the tree.
"You did not paint me."

"Come back here, Snake!" shouted Hippo.

"No!" said Snake.

"Please come here!" begged Hippo.

"No!" said Snake.

Just then, Lion came by.

More animals came by and stood next to the tree.

"Do you need any help?" they asked.

Hippo looked at all the animals standing next to the tree.
Then he looked at his painting.
"I give up," he said.

He tossed his brush into the air and walked away.

"Why did Hippo give up?"
asked Lion.

"He was having a hard time
with his painting," said Snake.

"Let's look at it," said Elephant.

All the animals walked away
from the tree and went to look
at the painting.

They looked at the grass and the
flowers, the hill and the sky,
the sun and the cloud, the
tree and the robin.

"I do not know why Hippo
was having a hard time,"
said Elephant.

"His painting looks perfect
to me!"

1. Why did Hippo have a hard time with his painting?

2. What did Snake want Hippo to paint in the picture?

3. When did you know that Hippo was mad at Snake?

4. What made Hippo give up painting?

5. Why do you think Snake did those things to Hippo?

*Alexander Calder's art makes
people feel happy.
Read to find out why.*

Alexander Calder

by Catherine M. Carroll

Alexander Calder was a great artist.
Alexander started making things
when he was five.

He made little toys and games.

He painted many pictures.

Alexander's mother and father
were artists, too.

They were happy that their son
liked to make things.

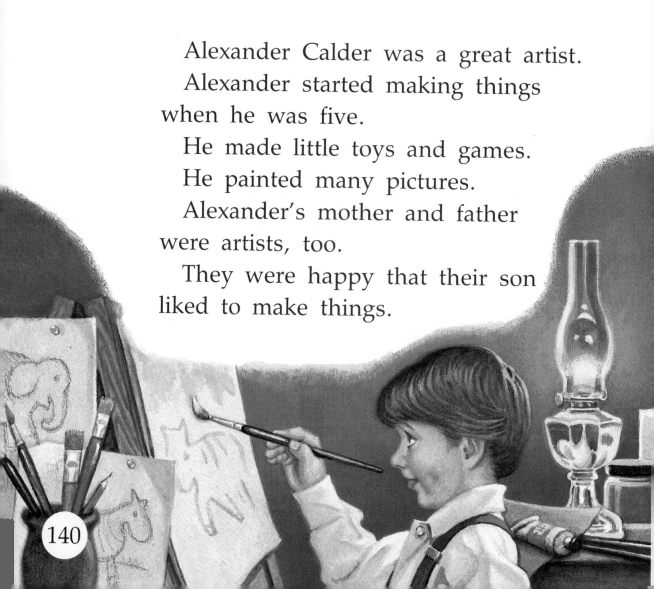

140

Alexander Calder liked to watch
the way things moved.

He loved watching how the animals
moved at the circus.

He drew pictures of circus animals.

When Alexander Calder grew up,
he made a toy circus.

People from all over the world
saw Calder's toy circus.

Collection of Whitney Museum of American Art.

Calder loved the moving toys
in his circus.

He wanted to make more
things that moved.

So he made children's toys
with moving parts.

Children loved to play
with the toys that Calder made.

Calder liked making mobiles
best of all.

Mobiles have many parts that move.
Some of his mobiles are very little.
Some are very big.

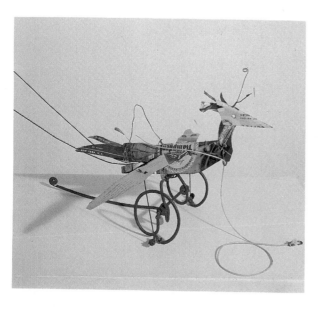

Calder liked to paint pictures, too.
He liked to use the colors red,
yellow, and blue in his pictures.
He liked these colors best of all.

Collection of Whitney Museum of American Art.

143

Alexander Calder was a very happy man.

He loved making things.

He said that his work was his play.

He thought that art should be happy.

He wanted his art to make people feel happy, too.

People laugh and smile when they see Calder's art.

1. Why does Alexander Calder's art make people feel happy?

2. As a little boy, what did Calder like to watch?

3. Name some things Alexander Calder made that you would like to see.

4. Why was Calder a happy man?

5. How do you know that Calder was an artist for a long time?

Thinking About "Smiles"

You have read about people and animals who have helped others.

Who were some of the people and animals that you read about?

What were some of the things they did to help?

Why did David's father smile?

Why did Mama Fig smile?

Why do people smile when they see Alexander Calder's art?

The people and animals in the stories were happy when they helped others to smile.

Which stories made you smile?

1. In the stories that you read, who made others smile?
   How did they do this?

2. How can you tell that the Sheep and Snake were not the same kind of friend?

3. How are Hippo and Alexander Calder the same?

4. Which stories that you read could not be true? Why?
   Which stories that you read could be true? Why?

147

Read on Your Own

Who's in Rabbit's House? A Masai Tale
by Verna Aardema. Dial.
Someone is in Rabbit's house and
won't let her in!

Like Nothing at All by Aileen Fisher.
Harper. In this book, you will
find that if you look closely,
there is a lot to see in a forest.

The Little Red Hen by Paul Galdone.
Clarion. Who will help the Little
Red Hen make her bread?

Herman the Helper by Robert Kraus.
Windmill. Herman, the octopus,
spends all day helping others.

I Am a Big Help by Marian Parry. Greenwillow. A mouse tells many ways to be helpful.

The Tale of Peter Rabbit by Beatrix Potter. Warne. In this book, you will enjoy reading about the adventures of Peter Rabbit.

It's Me, Hippo by Mike Thaler. Harper. In this book, you will find the story "Hippo Paints a Picture," along with more stories about Hippo.

A Special Trade by Sally Wittman. Harper. This book is about two good friends who help each other.

Long Ago

In "Long Ago," you will read about some things that happened long ago.

A little boy's grandfather will tell you about things that happened just a little at a time.

You will read about some very old and very big trees.

You will meet people who made things out of trees.

As you read, look for things that happened long ago.

Look for things that happened just a little at a time.

A lamb has a question about who is the strongest. Read the play to find the answer to the lamb's question.

The Strongest One of All

by Mirra Ginsburg

These are people who are needed for the play.

Narrator	**Cloud**
Lamb	**Rain**
Ice	**Earth**
Sun	**Grass**

Narrator: A little lamb slipped and
bumped his head on the ice
one day.

Lamb: Ice, Ice, you made me fall.
Are you strong?
Are you the strongest one of all?

Ice: If I were the strongest, would
the sun melt me?

Narrator: The little lamb went to the sun.

Lamb: Sun, Sun, are you the strongest one of all?

Sun: If I were the strongest, would the cloud hide me?

Narrator: The little lamb went to the cloud.

Lamb: Cloud, Cloud, are you the strongest one of all?

Cloud: If I were the strongest, would I turn into rain?

Narrator: The little lamb went to the rain.

Lamb: Rain, Rain, are you the strongest one of all?

Rain: If I were the strongest, would the earth swallow me?

Narrator: The little lamb went to the earth.

Lamb: Earth, Earth, are you the strongest one of all?

Earth: If I were the strongest, would the grass push its roots down into me?

Narrator: The little lamb went to the grass.

Lamb: Grass, Grass, are you the strongest one of all?

Grass: If I were the strongest, would a lamb eat me?

Narrator: The little lamb jumped up and laughed.

Lamb: I may slip and bump and fall, but I'm the strongest! I'm the strongest of them all!

1. What was the answer to Lamb's question?

2. Why did Lamb think that Ice was strong?

3. After that, what does Lamb want to know?

4. Who does Lamb ask in the story?

5. What does Lamb say when he learns the answer to his question?

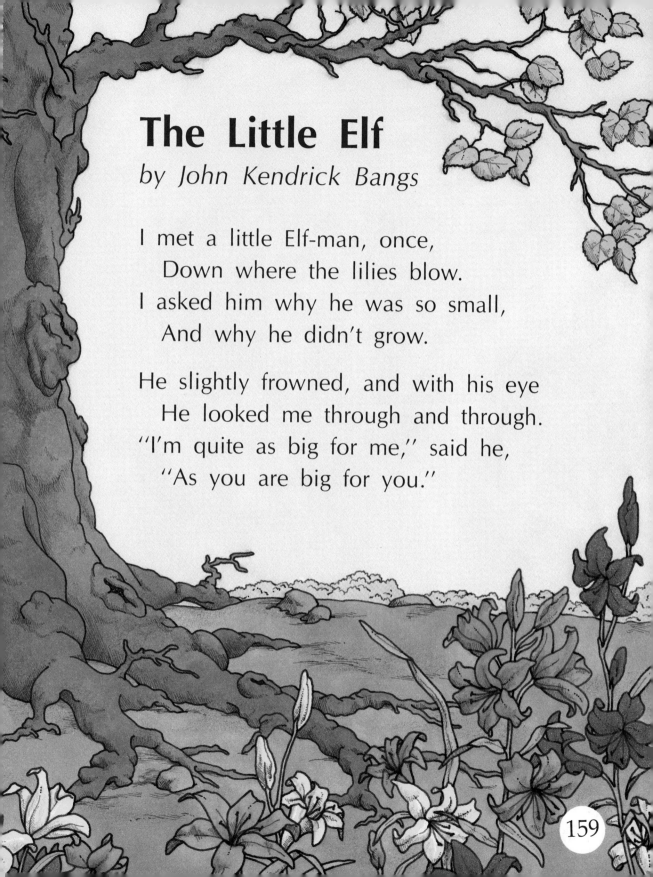

The Little Elf

by *John Kendrick Bangs*

I met a little Elf-man, once,
  Down where the lilies blow.
I asked him why he was so small,
  And why he didn't grow.

He slightly frowned, and with his eye
  He looked me through and through.
"I'm quite as big for me," said he,
  "As you are big for you."

In this story, a little boy learns many things from his grandpa. What does the little boy learn?

A Little at a Time

by David A. Adler

"How did that tree get to be so tall, Grandpa?" I asked.

"How did it get so tall?"

"When it started, it was just a seed. Then the seed grew and grew. It only grew a little at a time," Grandpa said.

"Why am I so small?" I asked.

"I used to be small like you,"
said Grandpa.
"You'll grow.
You will not grow as tall
as that tree.
You'll grow the way I grew,
a little at a time."

"How did this town get to be so big?

Were the buildings here always this tall, Grandpa?" I asked.

"All the buildings here used to be small.

As more room was needed, the small buildings were taken down.

Then these tall buildings were put up on the same land.

A town like this gets big, a little at a time," Grandpa said.

"Grandpa," I asked, "why is
this street so dirty?
Was it always like this?"

"Many people drop things,"
Grandpa told me.
"Each person may drop only a little.
This street became dirty, just a little
at a time."

"Look at all these steps, Grandpa.
See how fast I can get to the top!"
I said.

"If you run to the top, I'll be
left back here.
Walk the way I walk, a little
at a time," Grandpa said.

"Grandpa, what is this?" I asked.

"These are dinosaur bones.
It took a long time to put the dinosaur bones together.
People dug up the bones and cleaned them.
Then they had to learn where each bone fit.
It was hard work," said Grandpa.

"I know how they did it, Grandpa," I said.
"They did it, a little at a time!"

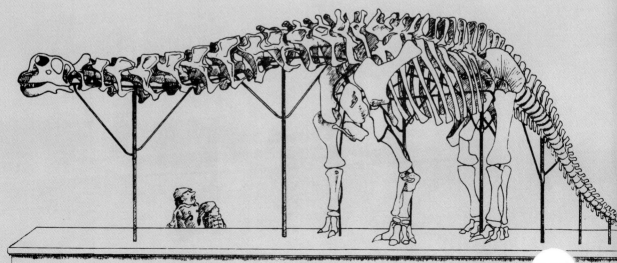

"How did you get to know so much, Grandpa?" I asked.

"I'm just like you!
I ask many questions.
Little by little I have learned a lot.
As long as I keep asking, I'll keep learning, a little at a time.
Now it's time to start going home," said Grandpa.

"How did it get to be so late, Grandpa?" I asked.

"You know the answer to that!" Grandpa said.
"The day went by, a little at a time."

1. What did the little boy learn from his grandfather?

2. How do many things happen in the world?

3. What things grew a little at a time?

4. How did Grandpa get to know so much?

5. When did you know that the little boy was telling this story?

Long ago, the giant sequoia trees were just little seeds. Find out what is happening to these trees today.

The Giant Trees

by Emily J. Knowles

The sequoia trees are very special trees.
They are very tall trees.
They are very old trees.
They are very pretty trees.
They are the biggest living things!

How did they grow to be so big?

The sequoia trees started
as little seeds many years ago.
The little seeds grew into
tiny plants.
The tiny plants grew into trees.
Each year the trees grew
bigger and bigger.
After many, many years,
they became giant trees.

5 years   25 years   75 years   1,000 years   3,000 years

People were surprised when they first saw these giant trees in California.

They knew that they could get a lot of wood from these giant trees.

They wanted to use this wood to make things.

Many sequoia trees were cut down.

After the trees were cut down,
their stumps were left in the forest.
One day, some people found the
stump of a giant sequoia tree.
This stump was so big that many
people could get on it at one time.

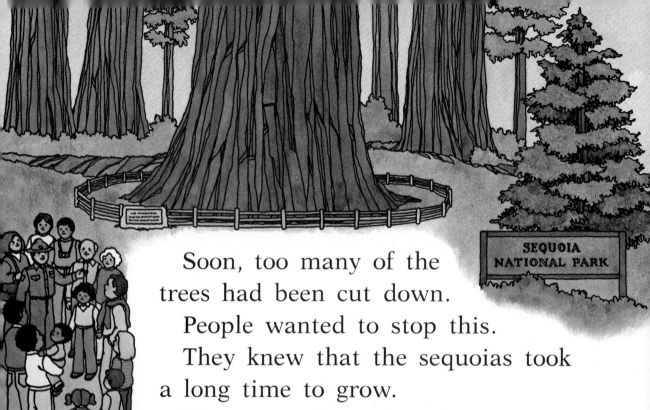

Soon, too many of the
trees had been cut down.
People wanted to stop this.
They knew that the sequoias took
a long time to grow.
They wanted to save the trees.

Now the sequoia trees are being
saved.
Each year, many people come to
California to see these giant trees.
They know that the sequoias
are very old and very special trees.

The sequoias are the biggest trees
in the world.
They got to be this way, a little
at a time.

1. What is happening to the giant sequoia trees today?

2. How did sequoia trees start many years ago?

3. What happened to many of the giant trees?

4. What in the story told you that it took the sequoia trees a long time to grow?

5. How were they saved?

Daisy finds something that her grandpa gave her father long ago. What surprise will Daisy's father give to her? Why?

Daisy's Surprise

by Dolly Cebulash

As Daisy was helping her father clean, she found a tiny canoe.

"Look at this canoe, Dad," she said. "It looks just like your big canoe."

Daisy's father laughed.

"So it does," he said, "but this canoe is much smaller.

Your grandpa gave me this canoe when I was a little boy."

174

"Why did Grandpa give you this toy canoe?" asked Daisy.

"Your grandpa took me fishing in his canoe many years ago," said her father.

"We didn't catch any fish that day. But we had a good time.

The very next day, he made me this smaller canoe out of wood.

He said that when I looked at the canoe, it would make me think of that day."

"Does it make you think of that day, Dad?" asked Daisy.

"Oh, yes," said Daisy's father.
"I'd like to take you fishing sometime just as Grandpa used to take me.
Would you like to go fishing with me, Daisy?"

"Oh yes!" said Daisy.
"I hope that we can go soon!"

The very next morning, Daisy's father put the canoe on the truck.
Daisy helped her father make lunch and put the fishing things in the truck.
Then Daisy and her father waved good-bye to her mother as they rode away in the truck.
Before long, they were at a pond.

Daisy got out of the truck and looked
at the pond.

She looked at the tall trees near
the pond.

She heard the wind in the trees.

"What a pretty place," said Daisy.

"Yes, it's very nice here," said Daisy's
father as he took the fishing things out
of the truck.

Daisy and her father got into the canoe and went out on the pond.

They sat in the canoe for a long time, waiting to catch some fish.

Sometimes they talked.

Sometimes they just watched and waited.

"This is like the day you went fishing with Grandpa and didn't catch any fish!" Daisy laughed.

Just then a fish jumped up out of the water.

"You've got a fish," Daisy's father said.
He helped Daisy pull it in.
Daisy looked at the fish.
It looked sad.
Daisy's father got a long string.
He tied the fish to the string.
Then he gave the end of the string
to Daisy.

"Now you can pick up the fish," her
father said.

Daisy held the end of the string and
looked at the fish.
The fish was trying to get away.
"I want to let it go," Daisy said.

"I thought you wanted to catch a fish," said Daisy's father.

"I did," said Daisy, "but I wanted this day to be like the day you had with Grandpa."

"I see," her father said as he helped her take the fish off the string.

They dropped the fish back into the water and watched it swim away.

Soon it was time to go home.

Daisy and her father laughed about the fish as they rode home.

Daisy went right to sleep that night. It had been a nice day!

The next day, when Daisy's father came home from work, he had a surprise for her.

It was tied with string.

"Open it," he said.

Before Daisy opened it, she said, "I think I know what it is.

It's a small canoe."

Her father just laughed.

When Daisy opened the surprise, she laughed, too.

"Oh, Dad," said Daisy, "it's not a canoe.

It's a toy fish, just like the fish I got at the pond."

"When you look at this fish, I hope you will think of our day," said her father.

"Thank you, Dad!" Daisy said as she hugged her father.

"This will always make me think of our day at the pond!"

1. What surprise did Daisy's father give her? Why?

2. Why did Daisy's father get a present from Grandpa?

3. Why did Daisy let her fish go?

4. Why do you think Daisy was surprised when she opened her present?

5. How do you know Daisy was happy with her present?

American Indians made canoes
many years ago.
How did they make them?

A Better Way

by Marie L. Smith

Long ago, many American Indians
lived near water.

They wanted to travel on the water.

They wanted to travel fast.

They also wanted to carry things
with them when they traveled.

The American Indians tried to find
a way to do these things.

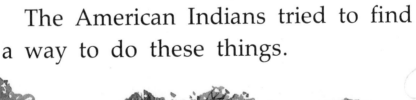

The American Indians saw logs
floating on the water.

They sat on the floating logs.

They used long sticks to help them
move the logs in the water.

Sometimes it was hard to stay
on the logs.

It was also hard to carry things
on the logs.

They soon found that using floating
logs was not the best way to travel.

The American Indians tried to find
a better way.

Then the American Indians
tied logs together to make rafts.

They found that they could carry
things on the rafts.

They could also fish from them.

But the rafts did not go very fast.

Sometimes the things on the rafts
got wet.

They soon found that using rafts
was not the best way to travel.

The American Indians tried again
to find a better way.

Now the American Indians
had another idea.

First, they looked for a log from a
big tree.

Next, they made a small fire
on top of that log.

Soon they put out the fire.

Then the Indians chipped the
burned wood out of the log.

They put the log in water and
sat inside it.

The log moved fast, and the things
they took with them did not get wet.

They had found a better way
to travel.

The American Indians
had made a canoe.

Today, canoes are still used.
Some people travel in canoes,
and some people use them just
for fun.

Many people are glad that
the American Indians found a
better way.

1. How did the American Indians make canoes long ago?

2. Why were floating logs not a good way to travel on water?

3. Why was the canoe a better way?

4. When in the story did you learn how canoes are used today?

5. If you were an American Indian who lived long ago, how would you have traveled on water? Tell why.

Follow Directions

Make a Paper Canoe

You just read two stories about canoes.

Now you can make a canoe out of paper.

You will need to follow directions carefully to make your paper canoe.

190

To follow directions, here are some
things that you will need to do.

1. Get all the things you will need.
2. Read each step of the directions
   carefully.
3. Start with step 1 and then
   follow each step after that.

Things you will need:

scissors   paste   crayons

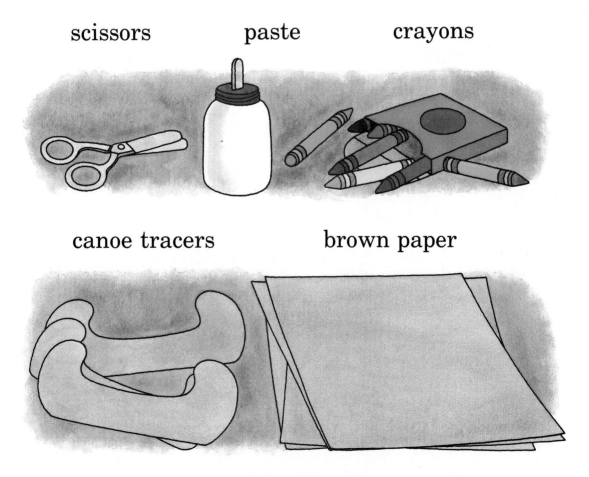

canoe tracers   brown paper

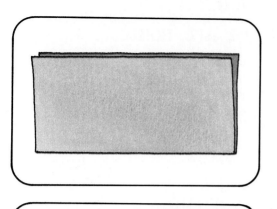

Now follow these directions carefully.

1. Fold the brown paper.

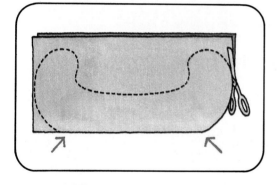

2. Put the canoe tracer on the fold and trace it.

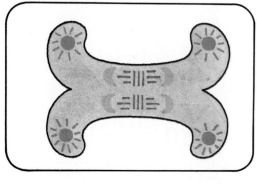

3. Cut out the canoe. Do not cut on the fold.

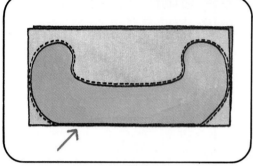

4. Open the canoe. Then draw pictures on the canoe and color them.

5. Turn the canoe over and put a little paste on the ends.

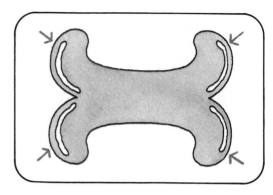

6. Put the pasted ends together.

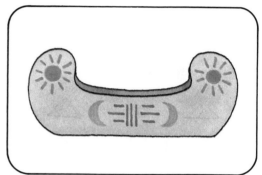

When you are finished, your canoe may look like one of these.

Sometimes there are better ways of doing things.
How do Frog and Toad find a better way to fly a kite?

The Kite

story and pictures by Arnold Lobel

Frog and Toad went out
to fly a kite.

They went to a large
meadow where the wind
was strong.

"Our kite will fly up and up,"
said Frog.

"It will fly all the way up
to the top of the sky."

"Toad," said Frog,
"I will hold the ball of string.
You hold the kite and run."

Toad ran across the meadow.

He ran as fast as his short legs could carry him.

The kite went up in the air.

It fell to the ground with a bump.

Toad heard laughter.

Three robins were sitting in a bush.

"That kite will not fly," said
the robins.
"You may as well give up."

Toad ran back to Frog.
"Frog," said Toad, "this
kite will not fly.
I give up."

"We must make a second try,"
said Frog.

"Wave the kite over your head.
Perhaps that will make it fly."

Toad ran back across the meadow.
He waved the kite over his head.

The kite went up in the air
and then fell down with a thud.

"What a joke!" said the robins.
"That kite will never get off
the ground."

Toad ran back to Frog.
"This kite is a joke," he said.
"It will never get off the ground."

"We have to make a third try,"
said Frog.
"Wave the kite over your head
and jump up and down.
Perhaps that will make it fly."

Toad ran across the meadow
again.

He waved the kite over
his head.

He jumped up and down.

The kite went up in the air
and crashed down into the grass.

"That kite is junk," said
the robins.

"Throw it away and go home."

Toad ran back to Frog.
"This kite is junk," he said.
"I think we should
throw it away and go home."

"Toad," said Frog,
"we need one more try.
Wave the kite over your head.
Jump up and down and shout
Up, kite, up."

Toad ran across the meadow.
He waved the kite over his head.
He jumped up and down.
He shouted, "Up, kite, up!"

The kite flew into the air.
It climbed higher and higher.

"We did it!" cried Toad.

"Yes," said Frog.
"If a running try
did not work,
and a running and waving try
did not work,
and a running, waving,
and jumping try
did not work,
I knew that
a running, waving, jumping,
and shouting try
just had to work!"

The robins flew out of
the bush.

But they could not fly
as high as the kite.

Frog and Toad sat
and watched their kite.

It seemed to be flying
way up at the top of the sky.

1. How did Frog and Toad find a better way to fly a kite?

2. What happened to the kite on the first try?

3. What did Toad want to do when the kite fell?

4. What did Toad always do after the robins talked to him?

5. What surprised you the most about Toad?

Thinking About "Long Ago"

You learned about some things that happened long ago.

You read a play about a little lamb who found out that he was the strongest one of all.

You learned how the giant sequoia trees started as little seeds.

You read about how the American Indians made canoes.

What are some things you read about that happened a little at a time?

What are some stories that tell about things that happened long ago?

1. What would grandpa in "A Little at a Time" tell the boy about the sequoia trees?

2. How are the stories "A Better Way" and "The Kite" the same?

3. How did the American Indians of long ago help Daisy's father?

4. How are the boy in "A Little at a Time" and the lamb in "The Strongest One of All" the same?

Read on Your Own

The Seasons of Arnold's Apple Tree by Gail Gibbons. Harcourt Brace Jovanovich. A boy enjoys his apple tree all year round.

Good Morning, Chick by Mirra Ginsburg. Greenwillow. All the farm animals try to teach a little chick something.

The Sun's Asleep Behind the Hill by Mirra Ginsburg. Greenwillow. The sun, a bird, a child, and others have a very busy day.

Days with Frog and Toad by Arnold Lobel. Harper. In this book, you will find the story "The Kite," along with more Frog and Toad stories.

Grasshopper on the Road by Arnold Lobel. Harper. A grasshopper meets some odd creatures along a road.

If the Dinosaurs Came Back by Bernard Most. Harcourt Brace Jovanovich. A boy tells what might happen if the dinosaurs came back.

Boats by Anne Rockwell. Dutton. In this book, you can read about all kinds of boats.

A Tree Is Nice by Janice May Udry. Harper. A tree is nice to hang a swing on. It's also nice to rest under. This book tells many reasons why a tree is nice.

Word Helper

"Word Helper" develops readiness for dictionary skills and provides students with a reference for words they may wish to use in their writing. An example sentence for new words in this book is given. Illustrated sentences are followed by ■

Aa

ad	He put the **ad** in the newspaper.
airplane	She flew the **airplane.**
anthill	The ants made a big **anthill.**
artist	An **artist** may draw or paint. ■

Bb

best	This is the **best** playground in town.
bone	The dog hid the **bone.** ■

broke	I **broke** my balloon.
brush	He painted the house with a **brush.** ■
build	The boys will **build** a plane.
buildings	Did you see the tall **buildings?**
bump	He will **bump** into the cart.
burned	The old tree **burned** down.
bush	The **bush** has red flowers.
butterfly	I saw a **butterfly** on a flower. ■

Cc

California	There are nice parks in **California.**

canoe　They went down the river in a **canoe**. ∎

carry　We can **carry** the canoe.

catch　She will **catch** a fish.

cave　The bear will stay in the **cave.**

chipped　He **chipped** at the wood to make a canoe.

circus　The clown did tricks at the **circus.**

cracker　He had a **cracker** for the duck. ∎

crash　When the tree fell, there was a **crash.**

crumbs　Some fish eat **crumbs.**

Dd

deep　He jumped in the **deep** hole.

dinosaur	This story is about a **dinosaur.**
dolphin	We saw a **dolphin** at the marine park. ■
drew	He **drew** pictures of animals.
dug	She **dug** a hole for the seeds.

Ee

earth	The **earth** near the tree is hard.
eat	What do you want to **eat** for lunch? ■
ends	The dog looked at both **ends** of the log.

Ff

fast	The horse went **fast.**

finished	I have **finished** reading the story.
float	The log will **float** down the river.
fold	You can **fold** a newspaper to make a hat. ■
forest	There are many trees in a **forest.**
funny	The clown did a **funny** trick.

Gg

giant	An elephant is a **giant** animal. ■
grow	Flowers **grow** best in the sun.

Hh

heard	We **heard** a peacock.

hook He put a **hook** on the end of his fishing pole. ■

hot The sun made us feel **hot.**

Ii

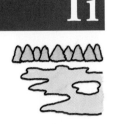

ice There was **ice** on the pond. ■

idea You had a good **idea.**

Jj

job His **job** was to drive the bulldozer. ■

joke He laughed at the **joke.**

Ll

lamb The mother sheep looked for her **lamb.** ■

laughter Their **laughter** told us they were happy.

learn	We **learn** many things at school.
 **lion**	Many zoos have more than one **lion.** ■

Mm

mail carrier	The **mail carrier** had a letter for us.
 **map**	He drew a **map** of the town. ■
marine park	We saw dolphins at the **marine park.**
meadow	Many flowers grew in the **meadow.**
 **mobile**	A **mobile** has parts that move. ■
morning	The sun comes up in the **morning.**

mud	There is **mud** near the pond.

Nn

net	The boy fishes with a **net.** ■
newspaper	I read the **newspaper** this morning.

Oo

otter	People came to see the **otter.** ■

Pp

path	We walked down the **path.**
peacock	People like to feed the **peacock.** ■

pelican	The **pelican** gets fish with its mouth.

plants	He put many **plants** near the house. ■
playground	They played at the school **playground.**
post office	The letter is at the **post office.**
prevent	We must **prevent** forest fires.

Qq

question	You can ask your **questions.** ■
	You can **question** us now.

Rr

raft	People will ride a **raft** down the river.

ranger The **ranger** works in the forest. ■

right That is the **right** answer.

roots The **roots** of the plant went deep into the ground. ■

Ss

save The dog will **save** the bone.

sea The boat followed the river to the **sea.**

sequoia The **sequoia** is a very tall tree. ■

shark A **shark** is a big animal.

shoulders He sat on the man's **shoulders.**

slid	We **slid** down the hill.
slip	Try not to **slip** on the ice.
smile	People **smile** when they are happy.
	She has a big **smile**.
someday	We will go to the zoo **someday.**
sort	He will **sort** the newspapers.
starfish	**Starfish** live in the sea. ■
stick	I found a **stick** on the ground.
stomach	The food will go to your **stomach.**
strong	They used a **strong** rope to pull the cart.

stump   A robin rested on the tree **stump**. ■

swim   Sharks and dolphins **swim** in the sea.

Tt

talk   I like to **talk** to my friend.

thought   She **thought** the smoke was from a fire.

throw   She can **throw** a ball very far.

tied   He **tied** the string to the kite.

toad   The **toad** sat in mud. ■

told   He **told** me about the parade.

trace	You can **trace** the picture.
tracers	The **tracers** will help you make the picture.
train	She will **train** the animals.
travel	We will **travel** in the van. ■
treetop	There is a bird up in the **treetop.**
truck	Put the boxes on the **truck**.

Uu

 **under**	The shark swam **under** water. ■

Ww

water	We took the boat out of the **water.**
waves	We saw **waves** on the sea.
	He **waves** at us from the boat.
web	There is a bug in the **web.**
wide	The new road is very **wide.**
wind	The **wind** blew very hard.
woke	I **woke** up in the morning.

wood	The door is made of **wood.** ■

world   People came from all over the **world.**

worm   The **worm** went down into the hole.

Yy

year   This **year** my brother will go to school. ■

Zz

ZIP code   Do you know your **ZIP code?** ■

Word List

The following words are introduced in this book. Each is listed beside the number of the page in which it first appears.

225

228

7
8
D 9
E 0
F 1
G 2
H 3
I 4
J 5